HOW IT WORKS

REFUSE COLLECTION

James Nixon

W

First published in 2009 by
Franklin Watts
338 Euston Road
London NW1 3BH

Franklin Watts Australia
Level 17/207 Kent Street
Sydney NSW 2000

Copyright © 2009 Franklin Watts

ISBN: 978 0 7496 8408 2

Dewey classification number: 363.72'8

A CIP catalogue record for this book is available
from the British Library.

Planning and production by Discovery Books Limited
Editor: James Nixon
Designer: Ian Winton
Commissioned photography: Bobby Humphrey

Photographs: Alamy Images: pp. 10 (Annette Price/H2O Photography),
11 bottom (Vince Bevan), 23 top (Jeff Morgan), 23 bottom (Chris
Photography), 24 bottom (Laurens Smak); Discovery Picture
Library/Chris Fairclough: pp. 9 top, 14, 15 top, 19 bottom, 22 top, 25
middle; Getty Images: pp. 20 top (Tim Smith), 25 middle (David H.
Silverman); Istockphoto.com: pp. 11 top, 18 top (Shaun Lowick), 19
middle, 22 middle, 21 bottom (Lai Leng Yiap), 27 left (Naigel Spooner);
Science Photo Library: pp. 16 (Silvere Teutsch/Eurelios), 17 (Robert
Brook); Shutterstock: pp. 6 top (Mike Flippo), 6 bottom, 8 top (Vadim
Kozlovsky), 9 bottom (Dusan Zidar), 12 (Dr. Morley Read), 13 top
(Michael Zysman), 13 bottom (Malibu Books), 15 top,
15 bottom (Images Hunter), 20 bottom (Perov Stanislav), 21 top, 22
bottom (Marcio Bastos), 25 top (Shutterlist), 27 top, 27 bottom.

Cover photos: Istockphoto.com: top, bottom right (Majoros Laszio);
Shutterstock: title background (Petr Nad), bottom (Vadim Kozlovsky).

Printed in China

Franklin Watts is a division of Hachette Children's Books,
an Hachette UK company.
www.hachette.co.uk

Contents

Words in bold are in the glossary on page 28.

A load of rubbish

Think about all the rubbish you create. What do you do with your rubbish?

What happens to the packaging on the food you buy from the shops?

What do you do with last week's newspapers and magazines? What about the clothes you have grown out of? You probably throw all of these things away.

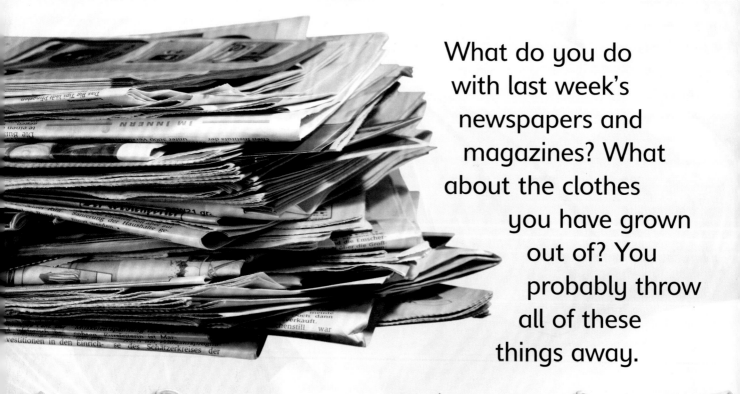

Putting the rubbish out

The sacks of rubbish you fill with all sorts of waste are tied up and left outside your house in a bin or on the street for collection. Your rubbish is then taken away in a truck. That is probably the last time you think about your rubbish. Have you ever wondered where it goes next?

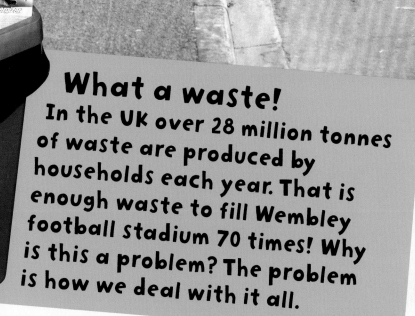

What a waste!

In the UK over 28 million tonnes of waste are produced by households each year. That is enough waste to fill Wembley football stadium 70 times! Why is this a problem? The problem is how we deal with it all.

Collection day

Do you know how often your rubbish is collected? Most houses have their rubbish picked up every week, or once every two weeks.

Refuse collectors come to your front gate and empty your rubbish into the back of their truck.

Wheelie bins

In some places every house has a wheelie bin outside to store their rubbish sacks. Special refuse trucks can lift up the wheelie bins and tip the contents in automatically.

Once the rubbish is emptied into the truck a crusher squashes up the rubbish and **compresses** it so the truck can hold as much waste as possible.

My name is Darren

I collect waste that has been separated into different types. This is so it can be recycled.

Materials such as paper, glass and plastic can be recycled. I come and pick up the recycling on a different day to the normal rubbish.

METAL

GLASS

PAPER

To the landfill

So where do the refuse trucks take your rubbish?

After the refuse collectors have picked up all the rubbish that is not for recycling they take it to a transfer station nearby.

At the transfer station

Here the waste is squashed up again and put into huge containers. The containers are then loaded onto larger lorries, which take your rubbish to its final destination.

Containers

▶ **The containers at this transfer station are being loaded by cranes onto barges. They will be transported by river.**

Dump it

The most common place for your rubbish to end up is a **landfill site**. A landfill is a huge hole in the ground where rubbish is dumped.

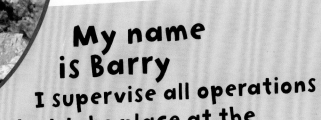

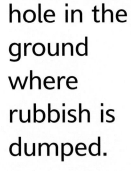

My name is Barry

I supervise all operations that take place at the landfill site. Landfill sites are divided into cells, which are filled in a certain order. I direct lorries arriving from the transfer station and make sure they dump their rubbish in the correct area.

At the landfill

Landfill sites are often old quarries, where rocks and minerals have been dug out of the ground.

Stopping leaks

Before the quarry can be used as landfill it must be lined with a thick layer of **clay**. This makes it waterproof and stops any harmful **chemicals** in your rubbish leaking into the soil.

Making it flat

Rubbish is tipped into landfill throughout the day. While this happens a heavy vehicle called a landfill compactor works to flatten the rubbish. It has spiked wheels to chop up the waste and a large metal blade on the front to push it into place.

Landfill compactor

At the end of the day the top layer of rubbish is covered with soil to stop it blowing away.

Golf course

Full up

What happens when there is no room left for any more rubbish in a landfill site? Usually the site is covered over with soil. You would never know it used to be a landfill! Grass and trees can then be grown on top of it. Some are turned to other uses, such as playing fields or golf courses.

Landfill problems

Dumping rubbish in landfill is easy and fairly cheap. However it does cause problems.

If we keep putting rubbish in our bins we will need more landfill sites. But space in landfill is running out. Nobody wants a new landfill site near their home because they are noisy, dirty and smelly.

Rot or not?
A lot of waste that is put in landfill is not **biodegradable**. This means it will not rot and disappear. **Manufactured** materials such as plastics are usually non-biodegradable. They can stay in landfill for thousands or even millions of years.

Poisonous rubbish
Landfill sites can cause **pollution**, too. Rainwater mixes with the waste and can sometimes seep through the clay lining into the ground. Poisonous chemicals can end up in rivers and streams if this happens.

Rotting rubbish produces a gas called methane, which also pollutes the environment.

Burning rubbish

Instead of going straight into landfill, rubbish can be burned in a huge oven called an incinerator.

The rubbish is heated to extremely high temperatures – around 1,000°C. The leftover ashes are cooled in water and then taken to a landfill site.

Burning rubbish reduces waste. However, harmful gases can escape from the chimney into the air, causing pollution. For this reason many incinerators have been closed down.

Incinerator

In the UK only a small amount of rubbish is burned. To build new incinerators that are cleaner and less polluting costs a huge amount of money.

Rubbish as fuel

The heat produced by an incinerator is used in some places to make electricity or heat homes. Even rubbish in landfill sites can generate electricity. The methane gas produced from rotting rubbish can be collected and used as a fuel in power stations (below).

Landfill site power station

Recycling rubbish

Another way to get rid of our rubbish is to recycle it. Recycling is about reusing materials to make new products.

We have seen how landfill sites and incinerators cause pollution. Recycling more will help protect the environment.

Don't chuck it!

Much of the waste dumped in landfill is not waste at all. It could be recycled and made into new things. Reusing materials also stops us having to manufacture new materials. This saves **energy**.

Local **councils** are trying to do more to help us recycle. Some homes are given special wheelie bins and boxes to fill with recyclable rubbish.

Recycling banks

You probably have a recycling site near your home.

GREEN GLASS

At sites like this there are banks for you to drop off glass bottles, paper, cans and maybe even old books and clothes.

Plastic Bank

Plastic Bottles Only

WHEN FULL PLEASE CONTACT COLLECTIONS ON: (01623) 721006

My name is Bev

I am a recycling officer. I inform people how to dispose of their rubbish and encourage them to recycle. I make sure refuse collectors empty the recycling banks when they are full.

Recycling plastic

Huge lorries take the rubbish you have recycled and carry it to recycling factories.

Sorting the plastic

Materials are often taken to a 'materials recovery facility' first (above). Here materials, such as plastics, are sorted into different types and colours. Each type of recyclable plastic has a different number in a triangle marked on it to make sure they are not mixed together.

Making new products

Once sorted, the plastics are made into bales and sent to the plastics factory.

Bale

There the plastic is shredded and washed. The plastic chips are then sent to a manufacturing plant where they will be melted and used to make new items, such as bin liners, carrier bags, food and drinks containers, toys and even shoes and coats.

Plastic chips

Why recycle?

It is important to recycle plastic if you can. Plastic does not rot and takes up space in landfill. Also, plastic is made from oil, a natural resource that is running out. Recycling plastic will save us using up a precious raw material.

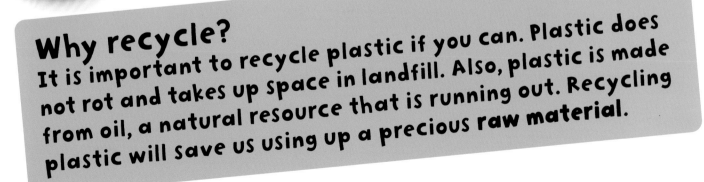

Recycling glass and metal

When your local bottle banks are full the glass is transported to the glass factory.

As good as new

At the glass factory the glass is cleaned and crunched up into bits. The bits are called cullet.

Cullet

The cullet is melted down to make new glass containers. Each new glass or jar will look as good as they did before!

Recycling metal

Lots of food packaging is made from metal, such as drinks cans, sweet wrappers and yoghurt tops. You can put all of this out to be recycled, too.

Before it is recycled metal is sorted into steel and aluminium at the landfill site or a materials recovery facility (right). The metals are then sent to a different smelting works (below) where they are melted down and made into new metal products.

Saving energy
The energy used in making a brand new aluminium can could be used to recycle 20 cans. If you don't recycle your drinks cans you are wasting energy.

Recycling paper

At the moment the UK is recycling around a third of its waste paper. Over half of the paper products you use at home will be made from recycled paper.

The best paper for recycling is white paper with little ink on it. This can be made into new writing paper. Newspapers and magazines are covered in ink so they are usually recycled into cardboard or newspapers again.

Pulp

Making a pulp

To recycle old paper, hot water is added to turn it into a mushy **pulp**. The pulp is then dried and pressed to make new products. The next magazine you read could be made from the Christmas cards you recycled last year!

Composting

You can recycle a lot of your food and garden waste yourself in a compost heap or bin. Paper and cardboard can be added to the heap as well. Over time these materials break down naturally and turn into a brown, crumbly compost. This is full of goodness and can be spread on your garden to help your flowers grow.

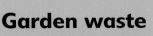
Garden waste

◀ Food and garden waste can also be put into separate bins that refuse collectors will pick up and take away to be composted.

Food waste

Reducing waste

Dumping waste in a landfill site is a waste of energy and resources and bad for the environment, too. Even recycling uses up some energy.

If we threw less rubbish away in the first place we would have less trouble disposing of it. Here are some ways you can reduce the amount of waste you put in your rubbish bins:

Make less waste

• Avoid buying things with lots of packaging. Items such as fruit and vegetables can usually be bought loose.

• Don't buy items that are designed to be thrown away, such as plastic cups and cutlery.

Reuse your waste

- Use both sides of a piece of paper before you throw it away.

- Always take a bag when you go shopping so you don't bring one home from the shop.

- Reuse a plastic drinks bottle by filling it with your drink every day.

Remember the motto – 'Reduce, Reuse, Recycle'. Throw as little away as you can, but if it has to be binned try to recycle it.

Glossary

Biodegradable Capable of rotting away naturally.

Chemicals Substances that have usually been created by people.

Clay A type of sticky earth that can be moulded together to make a waterproof layer.

Compost Decayed organic material that can be used to help plants grow.

Compresses Squeezes something so it takes up less space.

Councils A council is a group of people who run the affairs of the local area.

Energy The power needed to do and make things. Energy is used in the making of new products.

Fuel A substance, such as gas, which can be burned to provide heat or power.

Incinerator A furnace where rubbish is burned at high temperatures.

Landfill site A place where waste materials are buried in the ground.

Manufactured Made in a factory.

Pollution Something that makes the air, land or water dirty and dangerous.

Power stations Places where electricity is generated.

Pulp The substance made when paper is mashed with water.

Quarries Places where stone is removed from the ground. They are often later used as landfill sites.

Raw material The basic material from which a product is made.

Recycle To process used products so that the materials can be used again.

Further information

Books

The Recycling Centre (Out and About), Sue Barraclough, 2006 (Franklin Watts)

Recycling Materials (Making a Difference), Sue Barraclough, 2006 (Franklin Watts)

Recycling Officer (People Who Help Us), Rebecca Hunter, 2008 (Evans)

Reducing Rubbish (Making a Difference), Sue Barraclough, 2006 (Franklin Watts)

Rubbish and Recycling, Stephanie Turnbull, 2007 (Usborne)

Websites

www.recycling-guide.org.uk
This site shows you how to recycle a wide range of different materials.

www.go-recycle.org.uk
This site has all you need to know about recycling and contains quizzes and interactive activities.

www.recyclingconsortium.org.uk/primary
Here you can find out where all your rubbish goes. It also has tips on how to reduce, reuse and recycle.

Note to parents and teachers: Every effort has been made by the Publishers to ensure that these websites are suitable for children, that they are of the highest educational value, and that they contain no inappropriate or offensive material. However, because of the nature of the Internet, it is impossible to guarantee that the contents of these sites will not be altered. We strongly advise that Internet access is supervised by a responsible adult.

Index